CEL
CHRISTMAS

REV. JUDE WINKLER, OFM Conv.

Imprimi Potest: Mark Curesky, OFM Conv., Minister Provincial of St. Anthony of Padua Province (USA)
Nihil Obstat: James T. O'Connor, S.T.D., Censor Librorum
Imprimatur: ✠ **Patrick J. Sheridan, D.D.,** Vicar General, Archdiocese of New York

The Nihil Obstat and Imprimatur are official declarations that a book or pamphlet is free of doctrinal or moral error. No implication is contained therein that those who have granted the Nihil Obstat and Imprimatur agree with the contents, opinions or statements expressed.

CHRISTMAS DAY

IN the early days of the Church, no one was sure of when Jesus was born. So Christians in Rome chose to celebrate His birth on December 25, because the pagans already had a feast on that day when they celebrated the birth of the sun. This way, they might convince some of the pagans to become Christians. So we too celebrate Christmas on December 25.

For many of us Christmas is the happiest day of the year. It is a wonderful day when we celebrate the birth of our Lord Jesus Christ. In the weeks before Christmas, we decorate our Christmas tree and bake cookies and prepare a list of those things for which we will ask and those things we would like to give to our parents and brothers and sisters. Then on Christmas Day we go to Mass to begin our Christmas Day with God. When we arrive home, we open our Christmas presents and eat our Christmas meal.

Most of all, Christmas is a day to remember God's great love for us. We join with people from all over the world in giving thanks to God for His love. We thank Him for having sent His only Son into the world to be born as a baby in Bethlehem. But why do we do certain things to celebrate Christmas? Why do we have Christmas trees and Christmas cards? Why do we prepare a manger set? And who is Santa Claus and how does he belong to our Christmas celebrations?

THE CHRISTMAS TREE

ANOTHER Christmas custom that Christians have borrowed from the pagans is the Christmas tree. This custom was first practiced in Germany in the eighth century after Christ.

St. Boniface, a priest from England, had traveled to Germany to try to convert the pagans there. He had met with some success, but he was having a problem because many of the German people still wanted to worship their pagan gods.

St. Boniface wondered how he could convince the German people that the sacred oak worshiped by them was not a god. He finally decided that he would go into the forest and cut the sacred oak down.

The pagans were very angry when they heard of what St. Boniface had done. Now St. Boniface had to worry about how he would be able to calm them down.

Finally, he decided to give them a young evergreen tree as a sign of what Jesus was offering them. Unlike the oak that lost its leaves every year, the evergreen did not lose its leaves at all. This would be a sign of the life that Jesus was offering, a life that would never end. For the German people and for us, the Christmas tree is an important reminder of the gift God offers us in His Son: everlasting life.

HOLLY

IVY

MISTLETOE

6

CHRISTMAS PLANTS

THERE are also other plants associated with Christmas. Three of them come from England: holly, ivy, and mistletoe.

Holly has been used for hundreds of years to make wreaths that were hung on the doors of homes and in churches. Among some people, it was believed that holly had magical powers, for it was said to be able to keep witches away. But even more important is the fact that it was always seen as a reminder of the crown of thorns that Jesus wore when He was crucified. It is said that the red berries represent drops of blood that fell from Jesus' head.

Ivy has both a good and a bad meaning. For some, it was a sign of the pagan religions (for it is often made into crowns that were placed on the statues of pagan gods). The holly and the ivy were opposed (Christianity and paganism), and the holly won. Yet some speak of the white berries of the ivy as being a sign of purity and innocence.

The third plant, the *mistletoe*, had been used by the Celtic Druids (pagan priests) even before Christians arrived. They considered it to be sacred and used it in their ceremonies. So it was forbidden to use it in Christian churches. Yet it was often used in homes, for it was a charm to bring on marriage. To this day, there is a custom that one can kiss a person who is standing under a sprig of mistletoe.

THE YULE LOG

MANY other customs developed during the Middle Ages to celebrate this holy day. Some of them are still practiced, but others have slowly given way to newer ways of celebrating Christmas.

One of these customs is the Yule log. After the harvest, the workers on the great estates would go into the woods to find a great, thick tree trunk. They would cut it down and take home its widest part. When they arrived at the noble's house, they would soak the log in water to make it as wet as possible.

On Christmas Eve, the log would be taken into the noble's house and put in the fireplace. They would light a small fire under it, keeping the fire burning at all times. Because the log was huge and very wet, it would take a long time for the log to catch on fire and burn. As long as a part of that log had not yet burned, the workers did not have to go back to their work. This would take about a week.

Another medieval custom was to have a Christmas joust. All the Knights from a region would gather and practice their skills against one another as part of their Christmas festivities.

Finally, because Christmas was so holy, it was forbidden to do battle on Christmas and in the days surrounding it, for Christ is the prince of peace.

9

THE CHRISTMAS CRIB

ST. Francis of Assisi gave us one of the most beautiful Christmas customs. One December, St. Francis was staying in a cave on a hillside outside of a small town named Greccio. He always had a great love for Christmas and he wanted to help the townspeople celebrate it in a special way that year.

He asked permission of the Holy Father to put on a kind of Christmas play. St. Francis told the people of the town to bring their animals—their donkeys, sheep, and oxen—to the cave where he was staying. He also set up a crib as there had been in Bethlehem. Then the people celebrated their Midnight Mass to welcome in Christmas day.

During the Mass, St. Francis, who was a deacon, proclaimed the Gospel. He was so filled with love that the people who were there saw a vision in which St. Francis reached down and picked up the Baby Jesus, Whom they saw as alive and real. All of the people overflowed with joy and love at this great event, and it was said that they did not even need their torches to find their way home that night, for they were glowing with love.

The friars who followed St. Francis have spread the custom of setting up Christmas manger scenes all over the world.

CHRISTMAS CARDS

A NOTHER Christmas custom with which we are very familiar is the Christmas card. It is a great joy to send out these greetings and to hear from people whom we love but might not have seen for quite a while.

The earliest Christmas cards go all the way back to the fifteenth century. They were sheets of paper with the Christmas story printed on them, and they were not really the same things as the Christmas cards that we now send.

The first true Christmas card was printed in Britain in 1843 by Henry Cole. The center of the design is a Christmas feast with two scenes printed on either side of it that show Christians doing acts of charity. The card sent wishes for "A Merry Christmas and A Happy New Year to you." This first card was not very successful.

In the United States, one of the first Christmas cards was produced by Louis Prang in Boston in 1875. It was an immediate success.

Today, hundreds of millions of Christmas cards are sent each year. Some have pictures of the crib at Bethlehem or of Mary holding the Baby Jesus; others show a Christmas tree or a winter scene. But they all wish the people to whom we send them the joy of Christmas.

13

14

CHRISTMAS CAROLS

A LONG with Christmas cards, Christmas carols are one of the warmest memories that most of us have at Christmas time. In many cities, people still go from house to house, singing these simple songs that come from Europe and America. We hear their melodies in stores as we shop in the month of December. Every Christmas special on TV has our favorite singer or a chorus singing these wonderful songs. Then they are sung by the whole community as we gather for our Christmas Masses on Christmas Day and in the weeks after Christmas.

One of the most beautiful of these songs is "Silent Night, Holy Night." It was written almost by accident. Father Joseph Mohr, a priest from a small village in Austria, was getting his church ready for Christmas Midnight Mass in 1818. He discovered that the Church organ would not work. The mice had eaten out the cloth parts of the organ and it would not play.

Father Mohr was worried that there would be no music for Christmas. So he asked the schoolmaster, Franz Gruber, to set a Christmas poem he had written to music. Gruber worked on the song for the rest of the day, and then that night they sang their song, "Silent Night," to the music that he played on Father Mohr's new guitar. That night, Franz Gruber's wife turned to him and said, "I am proud of you! People will sing your carol long after we both are dead."

GOOD KING WENCESLAUS

A NOTHER beautiful carol that we sing at Christmas time has little to do with the Christmas story itself. The carol is "Good King Wenceslaus," and it speaks about a king who ruled long ago in Bohemia, which today is a part of Czechoslovakia.

Wenceslaus was born just about the time when the Catholic faith had arrived in Bohemia. His grandparents were both Catholic as was his father, but his mother, although she was baptized, really believed in the pagan ways. When his father, the king, died Wenceslaus was twelve years old—too young to be king. His grandmother cared for him for a while, but his mother had her put to death and tried to make him into a pagan. Yet the boy continued to read the bible in secret and sneaked priests into the palace to teach him.

When he was eighteen Wenceslaus became king. He ruled in a wise and just manner. He was famous for treating the simple people with respect and helping them. Often, when someone owed so much money that he and his family were about to be sold as slaves, he would pay their debts himself.

After Wenceslaus had ruled for only two years, the pagan nobles and his own brother plotted against him and had him killed. Yet the people so loved their king that they never forgot him and to this day they sing of their beloved good king Wenceslaus.

ST. LUCY

A NOTHER Saint who is associated with Christmas is St. Lucy. Her memory is especially celebrated in Sweden where her feast day, December 13, is a special holiday.

St. Lucy lived in Sicily in southern Italy during the days of one of the last Roman emperors who persecuted Christians. She is said to have hidden her fellow Christians underground in the catacombs (or tunnels where they would bury the dead).

Every night Lucy would climb down to bring them food. In order to be able to carry more food, she would carry her oil lamps on her head. Eventually, she was caught and put to death for being a Christian.

Her story was told in many countries, and in Sweden she became especially popular. They were very impressed with her service of others. The Swedes would speak of how her head was surrounded with a halo of light.

To celebrate her feast, a young daughter from each family gets up very early on December 13 and dresses up in a long white robe with a red sash around her waist. She puts on a crown of ivy that has seven candles in it. Then she wakes everybody up and serves them coffee and baked goods.

SANTA CLAUS

AND what would Christmas be without Santa Claus. Originally, Santa Claus, like St. Wenceslaus and St. Lucy, was a saint. His name was St. Nicholas, and he was a bishop of a city named Myra in Turkey. He lived in the early part of the fourth century and died on December 6 or 7 in the middle of the fourth century.

The most famous story told about St. Nicholas has to do with three young sisters who were very poor. Their parents were so poor that they did not have enough money for the daughters to get married. Nicholas heard about this and wanted to help them, but he did not want anyone to know that he was the one who was helping them.

Here the story is told in a few different ways. In one of the versions, he climbed up on their roof three nights in a row and threw gold coins down their chimney so that they would land in the girls' stockings, which had been hung by the fire to dry.

When the Dutch settlers came to the new world, they also brought their devotion to "Sinter Klaus" (St. Nicholas). In their legends, he was no longer pictured as being thin, but he began to look more and more like the Santa Claus that we know, with a jolly red face and a white beard.

THE "BEFANA"

CHRISTMAS customs are very different all over the world. While we speak of Santa Claus visiting our homes on Christmas Eve and dropping down our chimneys to leave us presents (as St. Nicholas did), other nations have different traditions about Christmas presents and who brings them.

In Italy, for example, Christmas is not even the day on which people receive presents. There, as in many other nations, presents are received on the feast of the Epiphany, January 6.

The Epiphany is the day when we celebrate the visit of the three Magi who came from the East to visit the Baby Jesus. They brought gifts of gold, frankincense, and myrrh with them to give honor to the newborn King of the Jews. Thus, it makes sense to give and receive gifts on that day to remember what the three Magi did.

In Italy, though, there is an interesting twist on the story. There, a good witch named the "Befana," visits everyone's home. Like Santa Claus, she knows who has been naughty and who has been nice. She brings gifts to all of the children who have been good throughout the year, but she leaves coal for those who have been bad. Her name, the "Befana," comes from the name of the feast on which she brings her gifts ("Epifania" in Italian).

THE "POSADAS"

IN Mexico, in the meantime, the nine days before Christmas Day are filled with Christmas celebrations. These days are called the "posadas," the Spanish word for lodgings or inns. Each of these meals stands for one of the inns in which Joseph and Mary stopped on their way to Bethlehem.

The evening begins as darkness falls. The children of the neighborhood carry three small statues: one of Mary on a donkey, one of Joseph, and one of an angel who is following them. The children all take a candle and sing hymns while they march in procession to the nearest house.

When they reach the house, they knock on the door and ask if Mary and Joseph can stay there for the night. If this is not the house for the "posada," they are told that everyone is asleep and they must go away. Finally, when they reach the chosen house, they are let in. They set up an altar decorated with their candles and flowers and they begin their nightly celebration.

There is food and music and dancing each of the nine nights of the "posadas." There is also a "pinata," a clay figure filled with candy and toys, which is broken open each night. A child is blindfolded and given a stick. The child tries to break the figure, and when it is broken, treats fall out and all the children rush to get their fill of the candy and other treats.

THE "OPLATEK"

W E have spoken of a number of Christmas customs, but there is one other thing that reminds us of Christmas: food. Christmas is a time when we come together as a family and share a large supper with many wonderful types of food.

Each nation has its own traditions that involve food. In England, for example, people eat goose and plum pudding. In Italy, there is a special coffee cake named the "Panettone" and a candy filled with nuts called "Torrone." In America, we have our Christmas cookies and fruitcake. Many families also have either ham or turkey for dinner on Christmas Day.

One beautiful custom involving food is found in Poland. There people bake pieces of bread that look almost like the hosts we use at Mass. They are called "oplatek," and each piece has a holy picture pressed upon its surface.

In the old days, people would carry their "oplatek" from house to house and wish their neighbors a Merry Christmas. Today, the bread is mostly shared with members of the family and immediate neighbors. As each person shares the bread, he or she is asked to do two things: forgive any hurts that have occurred over the past year and wish the person all the possible happiness in the coming year.

CHRISTMAS IN THE ORIENT

IN many parts of the world, it is not easy to celebrate Christmas. In countries where the government is communist, it is often illegal to take off from work on December 25.

Then, in other countries, Christians are only a small minority. In Japan, there are only about one half a million Christians in a country of 170 million people. Thus, many people do not even understand the meaning of Christmas. Christians use the holy day to tell their friends the story of Jesus.

In India, likewise, there are few Christians in comparison to the population. Yet the Christians of India have an advantage, for the Hindus, the major religion of India, have a Festival of Light called "Diwali," and Christians can use this festival as an example of what Christmas is like. In fact, they use some of the customs of that feast and other customs from the West to celebrate their Christmas.

One of the aspects of their Christmas celebration is also their Christmas Day service. It is a long service, usually lasting from two to three hours. The churches are filled with candles and flowers and the bright colored clothes of all the people. In some parts of India, too, people go from house to house singing Christmas carols all the night long.

30

THE TRUE MEANING OF CHRISTMAS

A S we read through these Christmas customs, we should be able to recognize some of the things that we do in our own country and some things that seem unusual to us. Because our ancestors have come from all over the world, we often have a mixture of customs that we follow — some from our own family and others from the families of friends.

One of the things that many people have complained about in recent years is that Christmas has become too commercial. People are worried about presents and cards and all the other preparations, but they forget the real meaning of Christmas. It is the birth of the Baby Jesus, God's message of love to each one of us.

Christmas should be spent in a way that reminds us of that message. We should tell the story of the birth of Jesus and sing about it in our carols. We should remember the true meaning of our Christmas tree and our manger sets. We should say a quick prayer every time we wish someone a Merry Christmas.

We should thank God for our families and remember that they are God's greatest gift to us. We should also remember those who are not as fortunate as we are because they are poor or homeless, and maybe we should think of sharing some of our gifts with them.

CHRISTMAS EVERY DAY

A FTER seeing all these customs from around the world, we can see there are many, many ways to celebrate Christmas. Whatever we do, it should help to remind us that Jesus cares so much for us that He was born in a manger out of love for us.

We, like St. Francis, should be so on fire with love for God that everyone can see that Jesus is real and alive in our hearts. We should make every day a little Christmas.